# Broker, Trader and Money

# Manual for Make Money (easy) in International Trade

# 2da. Edition, April 2015

www.carloscaraballo.com
twitter: @ asesorcaraballo
e-mail: info@carloscaraballo.com

Author: Carlos E. Caraballo B.
Design: Carlos Caraballo
Layout: Carlos Caraballo

Part of the profits from the commercialization of this manual will be designed to support and help entrepreneurs in each country to be acquired.

# Gratefulness

First I want to thank God for always being by my side helping to overcome every learning situation that I have experienced, bless my fantastic family and the opportunity to acquire all this knowledge is now starting to show the world towards helping entrepreneurs and businessmen.

Thanks to my wife Lizbeth Montsant for your love, support, understanding and dedication .... Being more than wife, lover and friend. I love you.

Thanks to my children: Alessandra, Gregoria, Jonathan, Michael and Orlinda .... by being themselves and always understand..

Many thanks to my mother and my in-laws ...!

To All Thank you for Being ...!

*Carlos Caraballo*

# Index

Gratefulness ------------------------------------------5

Index -------------------------------------------------7

Introduction. ---------------------------------------11

That is a Broker ...? ------------------------------15

The Broker. -----------------------------------------17

Types of agents. -----------------------------------18

And a Trader, who is ..? --------------------------24

The Trader. -----------------------------------------25

Let's Make Money ----------------------------------31

As the broker make money. -----------------------32

Greed and flexibility. -----------------------------39

The SELLER and the BUYER. -----------------------44

What You Should Know ----------------------------48

International Trade------------------------------------49

Incoterms ------------------------------------------54

Basic Incoterms ------------------------------------58

Documentation Required. -----------------------------61

LOI: Letter of Intention-----------------------------65

Offers: SCO and FCO ---------------------------------67

ICPO: Irrevocable Purchase Order. -------------------71

The Letter Credit -----------------------------------74

IMFPA / NCNDA----------------------------------------81

Draft Contract---------------------------------------85

Now we do business and win money. -------------------88

Labor  Supply. --------------------------------------95

## Introduction.

Today are much speculation regarding who is a trader or a broker.

Each word has a particular meaning and is already classics and coined both concepts, but there are also a lot of confusion in some quarters regarding the activity of both, especially novice traders and entrepreneurs trying to perform these activities.

This manual will you clarify the main concepts and tools commonly used for such activities, the most common documentation, the terms most used, glossaries needed to know or at least take them into account when initiated in these activities trading.

Many types of broker, as well as various types of trader, we will be something colloquial to explain and in turn give them concepts and technical details to consider, in short it will be easier to understand how to be an international businessman and not die try ....!

All are greeted and given a warm welcome to this new manual, Brokers, Traders and Money ...!

*Carlos Caraballo*

# That is a Broker ...?

# The Broker.

Placing a basic concept :

- Broker: the individual or firm that acts as an intermediary between a buyer and a seller, usually charging a commission. It is also responsible for advising and counseling on issues related to the business. The office of agent or " broker " normally requires a license to practice but is not a limitation ... . !

# *Types of agents.*

- Energy Agent

- Agent Real estate

- Customs broker

- Insurance broker : A person who acts as an intermediary of one or more insurance companies , selling insurance contracts for its customers

- Stockbroker (financial, business or change): A person who advises or transacts equity and values in financial markets.

- Bookie: person that takes bets and performs intermediation or n between bettors.

- Travel Agent: A person who sells, advises and manages

the travel log ie acoustic contracted by clients.

- Talent Agent: A person who acts as an intermediary between a worker of the show or sport and an employer .

These are just some examples of agents or broker ..!

But in short and not to complicate a lot, *a broker is an*

*intermediary* ..! They can be given many labels and understand that some do not share my opinion ... but broker = Intermediate ....!

There are other types of broker not reflected so far as they are business broker (purchase - sale of companies) and broker of commodities or products, also sometimes called *"commodity broker"* to come to be the intermediary between buyer and seller "X" products.

This last is that we focus on this book , it is an incredible opportunity for everyone within reach, not just those that somehow are in relationships logistics, customs and transport, but it also anyone, distinction, you can exercise to achieve a substantial, independent income

and sharing their current activity
...!

*And a Trader, who is ..?*

## The Trader.

The word "trader" means "merchant".

Several types of trader , the stock market for example is one of the best known , but mean " Merchant " and n is understood that there are many sectors in which a trader operates

In our particular case really talk about the trader's business products as well as in the anterior segment discussed relating to commodities broker, we also have a trader for these cases, but what's the difference ...?

Actually both are merchants, the broker is the intermediary in the negotiations in this area and is understood that the trader is the one who has direct contact with the supplier or buyer if necessary..! confusing truth ..!

Look, the broker intermediary to be clearly not necessarily know a direct supplier or buyer, but the trader yes, the broker usually this is linked with other brokers or traders that if they have some direct contact, if providers have in their portfolio, producers and / or purchasers.

It's simple, a broker with direct buyer or seller and becomes trader of that specific product ..!

Of course, this is very colloquial way, the intention of this book is to explain in a simple way, you can call trader but highly recommended a document confirming you as such or lose credibility in the business environment and that would be very harmful to your future negotiations.

There are a number of formats and documents shall explain them so they can better understand and thus carry out this activity more easily.

If you realize, people working in logistics have link to many providers …. The brokers also, even, all carriers and companies that are acting as liaison between a buyer and a seller to simply speed up or complete a distribution network or transaction has incredible

potential in these businesses ...
Trader & broker. And without
leaving your current activity ....!

We do not dismiss the rest of
the concepts and activities of each
trader, only that we focus on trade
in products specifically
international level in this book.

# Let's Make Money

## As the broker make money.

Explained in a simple way the basics and the activities of broker and trader of products are interrelated and go on now with the money ....!

As we make money the broker and trader of products and as any of you can do from your home, office, or anywhere in the world, you just need some basic knowledge, a computer with internet access and mobile phone access details ..!

That's it, here we will give you the basics.

- The trader and broker products make money in much the same way, "commissions", it can be a fraction of the price, a percentage, a bonus, but in the end always is classified as "commissions".

Some trader to have direct customer do not like at all to do business with more intermediaries (broker) and yet many of them started their activities being just that, others things in life are trader directly, but in reality is not so bad doing business with intermediaries, one must sacrifice some of their own gain but I assure you there are very good broker to help them close one or several deals in no time.

*Then, as we make money ..?*

For each contract closing a broker the sale of a product previously agreed terms pay the seller commission for sale, it's like selling any product you see in the supermarket, it's the same principle, certain product offers, someone needs, you are in the middle and connect and concrete negotiating a commission is earned, that simple ..!

The difference is that in business transactions the broker and trader and commissions are at industrial level, only that, for example, instead of selling a kilo of flour from a full container sell up (thousand tons, Complete a boat, etc.) And so with any other product shipments, do not do business on a small scale, negotiate (almost always) a minimum of one full ship product and is actually simple.

And on average by one contract you can ensure a salary (minimum) at approximately $ 5,000 monthly.

As friends say power service, ca

*"SOMEONE HAS WHAT YOU*

*FIND SOMEONE ..... WHATEVER*

*YOU LOOKING ....!*


*WE TAKE CARE OF THE REST*

*.....! "*

## *Greed and flexibility.*

Continuing the above example the supermarket, for us the broker and traders of products the supermarket is the planet in general, our businesses do not stop by country, but we must know basic rules of international trade.

One of the evils to be avoided is greed ...!

In one contract you can earn from 1 to $ 10 "per ton" negotiated on average, of course, everything depends on the negotiations, the product, the type of contract and another variety of "basic" factors, but when one the team is placed in non-negotiable position on its committees most likely the business falls ...!

I have seen business more than $ 500,000 fall because a trader will not accept that the commission down $ 0.05 …!

However if we agree that we can win each and are flexible I assure you can close more deals in less time.

Then one of the main rules is that we "be flexible" in the agreements.

All this happens because our work does not increase the cost of goods as many people think, in this case the seller has already provided the amount payable commission, either to be divided between two intermediaries or more, but the amount with respect to product and buyer will not vary, of course, there are exceptions, but in general the seller places his margin and is on our side and bring to agree the best distribution of money.

# The SELLER and the BUYER.

Something very important: the seller is paying commissions to broker and trader, not the buyer, some few exceptions this rule is met in a high percentage of cases.

Most buying and selling operations that are performed by the broker contracts a minimum of one year, or at least is what is intended, that way ensure your income every month while you close the next deal and so on.

However, some customers request a single purchase and such purchase is called a "spot".

A spot is a single shipment of a particular buyer, but must be very city with spot applications, since many people use your negotiating a Spot to access your clients and then hire that way for 12 months but you leave you out in that agreement, just trying to pay you for the spot to prevent this case you should always try to contracts of six months or a year, but otherwise makes it clear parameters negotiation and writing.

Of course, as you will understand the price on a "SPOT" You can not be the same as a one-

year contract where they are
hiring 12 ships at a time ...!

# What You Should Know

# International Trade

Can you already possess some knowledge of international trade, but may not have a clue how to start with this manual can start in very short time and in a simple way in this exciting and lucrative international trade.

At the time of making an international business are a number of varied and diverse documentation, for each country there are different types of permisologías both to import and to export the same type of product.

In our case, you can review and study the different laws of each country on the subject of international trade at a particular time, or based on your expectations, but for now I'll say something very interesting: "You only need international standards Basic for broker ".

As a broker you do not need extensive knowledge of regulations and documents required in each country because of that the trader and the end customer is responsible, that is, you do the work of trading, to place the product or to find the supplier, monitor, etc. But the client is the one who then has full responsibility and obligation to have and do everything required by their government at the time of export / import.

Logically it is prudent to have basic knowledge of the documentation with countries hurdles to negotiate, but your knowledge is initially focus on international standards, which will be useful for dealing with almost any country.

# Incoterms

Clearly, there are a lot of international standards for all types of negotiation, but there is a group of terms that are most commonly used, indeed, are essential to know for any international business transaction, are "Incoterms".

*"The purpose of Incoterms is to provide a set of international rules*

*for the interpretation of the most commonly used trade terms in foreign trade. Thus, the uncertainties of different interpretations of such terms in different countries can be avoided or at least reduced to a considerable degree. "*

Here are some concepts necessary to understand when it comes to being a broker or trader trading products internationally, since according to its acronym may know whether a certain product will be negotiated to be paid in the same courtyard of the plant or factory ( EXW), or already embarked on the dock before leaving home (FOB) or once you arrive at your destination with paid freight and insurance (CIF).

These are just some examples of three of the most used in our business, of course, there are many more and these have evolved over time, so when you start the negotiation is very wise to have knowledge under which incoterms are going to work that particular product.

## Basic Incoterms

Here I put some of Incoterms recommend learning that there are more, but these are best used:

**EXW** = EX FACTORY means the sole responsibility of the seller, is to put your goods available to the buyer on his own premises.

In this mode, the seller delivers the goods in their establishment or at an agreed place to the buyer chooses the means of transport and bear the costs and risks inherent in the transportation of goods

**FOB** = Free On Board When the seller is responsible for placing the merchandise aboard a ship in the port indicated in the sales contract.

The exporter pays all related costs including insurance of goods, even physically put on board the vessel designated by the importer, shipping and land is used when it is trading at the border.

**CFR** = Cost and Freight The seller must make the clearance of goods for export and pay costs and freight necessary to transport it to the specified destination.

It is the seller who selects the shipping line and pay ocean freight to the named port and the loading of the goods to ship, like the customs export formalities. It is used in shipping.

**CIF** = Cost, Insurance and Freight CFR is a similar term, but in this case, the seller must also procure marine insurance for merchandise buyer.

It is up to the seller all necessary formalities for export, this term can be used in all types of transport.

## Documentation Required.

As every business transaction there are some necessary documents to finalize a comprehensive negotiation, as well as a national stock sale know invoices, purchase orders and quotes among others, there are also basic and standardized paperwork in international trade.

One recommendation: All documentation should be Emims or receive on letterhead of the company where the company name, address, website is included (if applicable), e-mail and telephone number as minimum data.

All documentation are primarily in English, hence the names based on their initials, we need to master basic documents are:

- LOI: Letter of Intention or n for its acronym in English.

- SCO: Soft Corporate Offer.

- FCO: Full Corporate Offer.

- ICPO: Irrevocable Purchase Order.

- LC: Letter Cr é dito.

- IMFPA / NCNDA: documentation or necessary to ensure the payment of commissions.

- Draft contract: draft contract to run.

# LOI: Letter of Intention

It is the formal listing application for a given product, in this as much product parameters expected purchase, as their characteristics, average prices (target Price), place of employment, among other specified.

These LOI are issued to gain access to the supply of product you need, is the way to start a serious business, but be careful, not all you request it have the product so you should take care not to issue multiple LOI to random, intends to issue LOI aimed at businesses, not individuals.

# Offers: SCO and FCO

These are the models most common deals that are used, the SCO: Corporate Offer Soft, as its name suggests is a soft offer and not have a lot of data or complete product parameters to bid, basically used to inform the potential buyer that a particular product has the initial details, such as the amount to be offered, the source port the same, the average price and other data, just basic.

If the buyer is interested in the product referred to in the SCO will then proceed to issue a LOI so that the supplier has basis for developing the FCO, which has been the full offer.

In the FCO if all product parameters are included to negotiate as:

1. Product Description:

2. Quantity:

3. Price:

4. Discount:

5. Professional Charge:

6. Payment:

# 7. Delivery:

# 8. Documents:

Updated product data sheet is included, suggested payment procedures, among others.

## *ICPO: Irrevocable Purchase Order.*

As its name indicates becomes the purchase order issued by the buyer with the intention of buying the product traded.

Its characteristics are very similar to the LOI, the main difference is that in the ICPO are already including banking parameters purchaser to be used in the draft contract to run and if necessary the can use the seller to verify the bank reference the buyer.

In many operations the parties directly issuing process forward FCO being answered with ICPO directly or vice versa and thus speed up the negotiation process.

This type of operation is very common among brokers or traders and experienced.

# The Letter Credit

There are several payment methods in these operations, the most used are the Charter credit and better bank transfers known as MT103, but even when the negotiation will be paid by transfer (MT103) a letter credit stanby used as collateral backing for the operation.

*Letter credit concept.*

-. Document issued by a bank acting at the request of a client and in accordance with their instructions undertakes:

- Make a payment to a third party or to the order, to pay or accept bills of exchange to free the beneficiary.

- Authorizes another bank to perform the above activities.

It is the most widely used means of payment in international trade, since the payment of the transaction is endorsed and guaranteed by a bank, which gives you more confidence and strength to negotiation.

There are various models Credit Card, always adaptable to the type of transaction and will normally be traded on the procedure suggested in both the LOI and the SCO.

Some features of Letter credit are:

**Type**

a) **Revocable,** can be modified by the issuing bank or the payer without notice to the beneficiary.

**b) Irrevocable,** the issuing bank will pay the loan provided that the beneficiary submits the required documents can not be changed without agreement between the payer and the payee.

- Confirmed, a confirming bank agrees to repay the loan if the issuing bank not to.

- No confirmed, there is no confirming bank operation.

**Modalities**

**a) Transferable**

- The recipient can instruct his bank for the credit to be used wholly or partly to one or more beneficiaries.

- Must include the clause transferable.

- Used when the exporter does not have the goods to be exported, assuming a guarantee of payment to suppliers.

**b) Revolving or Rotary**

- The loan is automatically renewed on the same terms and conditions as many times as specified.

- Used when the supply of the goods was partially done, so each credit is set to each of the various supplies.

- These partial credits may be:
Cumulative, the amount of credit not used in a period accumulates to the next.
Not cumulative, the amount not spent is canceled.

**c) With a red clause,** the exporter can benefit from a total or partial payment of the loan.

**d) With green clause** it is similar to the previous, but the exporter must prove possession of the goods or that this is in the process of manufacture.

# *IMFPA / NCNDA*

Are the initials in English of:

I RREVOCABLE **M** ASTER **F** EE **P**rotection **A** GREEMENT (IMFPA)

**N ON-C** IRCUMVENTION, **N** &
WORKING **ON-D** ISCLOSURE **A** GREEMENT
(NCNDA)

INTERNATIONAL CHAMBER OF COMMERCE
(ICC 400/500/600)

These are the documents endorsed by the International Chamber of Commerce to support you negotiated commissions are paid on the transaction.

In the same every negotiation parameters are described, including the product trade, quantities, prices, percentages and amount of fees and all beneficiaries, including their respective bank accounts.

This document must be entered in the bank so that each time a payment is made alluding to the contract the bank will automatically transfer you to your commitments outlined in the NCNDA account.

It is common that your counterpart in the business does not get the data of your direct customer before having signed this document, because you run

the risk of being left out in the
negotiations.

# Draft Contract

DRAFT CONTRACT TO
RUN.

This is the final stretch of the
friends negotiations, once they
have exchanged the above
documents, the offer, the bank
details have been agreed both
parties in the payment process,
and agree on all the parameters of
the negotiation both the buyer
and the seller, then the seller

proceeds to issue this draft final contract to be checked by the buyer.

This contract is still called draft it is to be checked by the buyer and is still subject to change.

In this draft contract all the details of the negotiations, clauses relating to the product, shipments, prices, commissions, brokers, payment procedures, etc. are reflected

This should be as comprehensive as possible in terms of the parameters of the negotiation, once you check the buyer manifest agree returning it to the seller signed and sealed on acceptance of the terms and proceeds to run.

*Now we do business and win money.*

Right now if you read through this manual and you must have the skills to make money in international trade.

As you have seen, is really simple this activity, you just need to want to do, a computer with internet access and the best ... you should not make any investment to start.

If you are decided or determined to earn money in international trade then the first thing is to follow some basic steps:

1. The organization and activity throughout the first step is to organize your new start, make your plans, goals and objectives to achieve short and medium term.

2. You need all the basic formats to start early negotiations, and are as follows:

- LOI
- SCO
- FCO
- IMFPA / NCNDA

With these formats only you can already start. Your email should powerservice27@gmail.co

<u>m</u> and we will send you free of charge.

3. You need a product to offer, either, recalls, "someone needs what you have." And in the wider world it is our supermarket someone needs the product you have.

This product you need all the important details:

- Quantities available

- Capacity of the factory

- Sale price

- No commission or margin

- Country of origin

- Port where the product will embark

4. Now that you have the format of the SCO, fill it with information about your product and send the offer to the buyer, no data from your provider, only the data of the product.

If you're going to start with relationships with other broker or traders recommend you do not give the name of your client to not advance the negotiations, **NEVER** give your customer data in the first conversation or meeting.

# Labor Supply.

"If you want to start making money with customers and proven aid and contact us by email *powerservice27@gmail.com* and for buying this book and be part of the team, we will send you both suppliers and sellers in a structured manner, and in this month you're closing your first international business. "

*If you already have customers and do not know how to proceed also hope for your contact, we have a very good proposal for you to win money in the short term.!*

So ... do business now and *Win Money ....!*

www.ingramcontent.com/pod-product-compliance
Lightning Source LLC
Chambersburg PA
CBHW070832180526
45168CB00002B/817